For Marilyn

AT LAST TO THE OCEAN

The Story of the Endless Cycle of Water

by JOEL ROTHMAN with photographs by BRUCE ROBERTS

CROWELL-COLLIER PRESS, New York/Collier-Macmillan Limited, London

Photographs from Rapho Guillumette Pictures.

Clouds begin to form.

High above the ocean,

clouds begin to form.

Darker and darker
they grow
as they float toward
the mountain tops.
Darker and darker.

Suddenly,
as thunder
booms,
they burst.

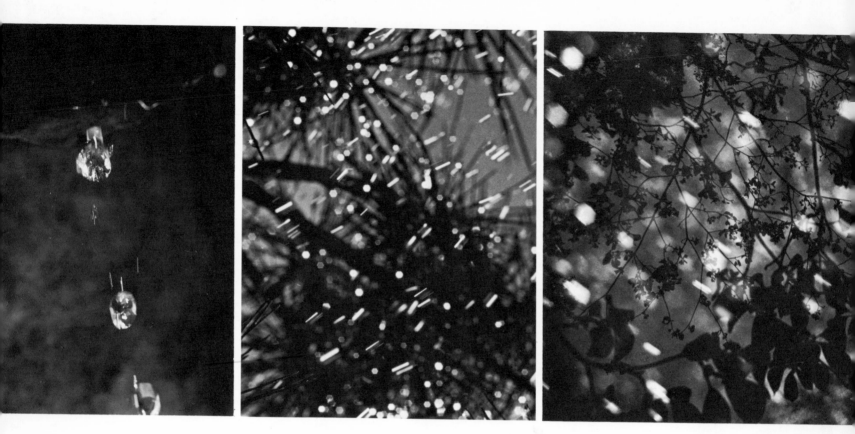

Rain begins to fall.
Over mountain tops
dark clouds burst,
and rain begins to fall.

Water trickles
down the mountains.
Streams begin to form.

Over mountain tops
rain is falling,
and streams begin to form.

Downward flow the streams,
over leaves and over earth,
over twigs, stones and rocks,

through
woods,
fields and
rolling hills.

Turning, twisting,

streams

of water

rush

to meet

the river.

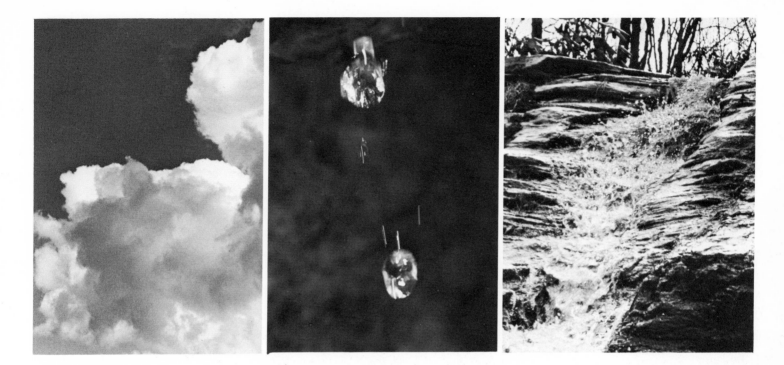

From clouds   to rain   to streams

...to the river.

The river swells
against its banks
as it meanders
across the countryside.
It carries water.

Water for drinking,

for swimming,

for boating.

Water to grow
plants and flowers.

Water for power to run machines.

Water —

in all its

beauty.

Onward runs

the river,

flowing

to the ocean.

From
dark
clouds

to rain

to streams   to the river

...at last to the ocean.

The heat of the sun
turns water into vapor.
Water constantly
evaporates,
invisibly rising.

Clouds begin to form.

High above the ocean,
clouds begin to form.